THE
DADA BASE+

Allen Brokken's
Most Popular Jokes
from Social Media
+

Crafting Jokes & Puns for
Kids
The Complete Course

THE DADA BASE+

THE DADA BASE+

Published by Towers of Light Christian Resources LLC, Towers of Light and associated logos are trademarks and/or registered trademarks of Towers of Light Christian Resources LLC.

Edition 1.0
ISBN: 978-1-962562-18-8

This is a work of parody and humor. Names, characters, businesses, places, events, and incidents are either the products of the author's imagination or used in a satirical manner. Any resemblance to actual persons, living or dead, or actual events is purely coincidental.

DEDICATION

To my Uncle Bob for always having the
keeping the puns rolling at
Thanksgiving alive

To all the parents looking for clean fun
for their kids.

I've got your back!

CONTENTS

ACKNOWLEDGMENTS

I want to thank my son Ethan Brokken for setting me on the road to putting my jokes online, my virtual assistant Heather Freeman for faithfully putting this all together, and Reace Erbe for her artwork.

PEANUT BUTTER

I ran into the construction foreman last night. They're gonna be putting in the street today, and I'm pretty excited about that. But he was carrying a case of peanut butter with him, and I was like, "What's that all about?" He said, "Well, in case there's a traffic... jam!"

I heard a rumor about peanut butter...
But I better not spread it!

Because if I told you the baker might...
get jelly!
Then I'd be ...
toast!
My son says this joke is ...
crusty!

FOOD
(TASTEFUL HUMOR)

My son tried to tell me this dad joke
about candy bars. It wasn't very
good...
So, I just snickered!

Have you seen that TikTok with the
Yeti giving diet advice?
Yeah, he says you really want to eat a
lot of iceberg lettuce!

Did you hear about the breakfast
cereal that went to the
gym twice a day?
It was some really shredded wheat!

When I was a kid, I really wouldn't eat my greens. So, one time my mom decided she would dress them up like a cowboy.
She thought I might eat them if they had a ranch dressing!

Did you hear about the Italian chef who got buried alive in spaghetti and meatballs?
The coroner's report came back, and it said he pasta way.

What do you call a yam on a lazy susan?
A rotato!

Did you know that ice cream can
receive an education?
It goes to sundae school!

I'm on a special diet that doesn't let
me eat spaghetti. I have to have
zucchini cut in the shape of noodles.
You know what my boys
say about that?
They don't like it; they say they're
impastas!

Why did the space rock eat a
hamburger?
He wanted to be meteor!

THE DADA BASE+

TRAVELING

I was traveling with my son. We were in the airport late for a connecting flight and he kept jogging on up ahead, and I could barely keep up.

He called back to me, "Come on Dad you need to go!"

Out of breath, I heaved, "Dude, I'm old!"

He replied "But look, there's Taco Bell, we should stop."

Confused I asked, "What do you mean stop? We can barely make it to the gate as it is."

He laughed "No Dad, it's perfect, it'll give you the runs!"

One of the cool things about taking off in flyover country is you see all these huge windmills.
Yeah, I'm a huge fan!

My son and I went to the Coca-Cola Museum last weekend and we found this lost baby Coca cola. And I asked him, "What's wrong?
Why are you crying?"

And he said, "I'm looking for my POP."

I was up at Disney World last night and the custodian was just laying down the dad jokes. It was awesome. Here's a good one. What did the janitor say when he opened the closet door? "Supplies!"

Back in the day, I was on the road for my son's fourth birthday. When I got home, I almost didn't recognize him. I'd never seen him be four!

I went to the Big Cats' Rescue shop in Florida. You know what I learned? If you ever lose your hat to the lion's cage, it's time to get a new hat!

So, my flight got delayed today and I checked with the gate agent, and I was like, "So what, is it raining cats and dogs in Philadelphia?" She was like, "No, there's no real weather there. All you might have to worry about there is hailing taxis!"

CHRISTMAS

So, I was talking to Santa the other
day, and he's proud of his first-year
little helpers.
They've all learned the elf-abet.

Did you hear Santa's Helpers have a
new band who are topping the charts?
They're the best wrappers!

So, I've got a good friend of mine. He's
got everything. He's so hard to shop
for at Christmas.
And then I thought about it and came
up with the perfect gift. He needs a
burglar alarm!

So, you know, after Christmas time Santa's usually pretty broke. Unless he stores some extra cash in a snow-bank!

Do you ever hear some weird noises in your house? Well, the other day I snuck up on the stamps and the Christmas cards having a conversation. The stamps were telling the Christmas cards, "Hey, if you stick with us, we'll go places!"

So, I was talking to a farmer the other day. I asked him, "What about the turkeys that make it past Thanksgiving? What are they called?" And he said, "Christmas dinner."

I was talking to Santa the other day, and I noticed just how bright and shiny his sleigh was. I said, "Santa! How much did that set you back?" He said, "Didn't cost me a thing. It was on the house!"

I was talking to my friend the other day. He's a meteorologist. I asked him, "Why is Christmas always so cold?" He looks at me without batting an eye and he says, "Because it's Decem-brrrrrrrr."

Why is it a bad idea to invite crabs to your Secret Santa?
Because they're shell-fish!

ANIMALS

Ethan and Sparkle Frog from the
Towers of Light Series

So, I heard about this cheetah. Its
owner put it in the shower twice a day.
Now, it's spotless!

I hear the LA Lakers are adding a duck
to their roster.
Yeah, he's going to be there to make
their fowl shots.

Did you hear about the skunk that fell
in the swimming pool?
He stank right to the bottom!

You know, I've never seen an unhappy frog.

I think it's because they just eat whatever bugs them.

Why do dragons like to eat sheep? Because it makes them feel all warm and fuzzy inside!

I heard about this turkey that tried to get out of being Thanksgiving dinner by joining the NBA. Didn't work out so well for him. He got kicked out of the league for fowl play!

Hey, remember that leopard from the Big Cat Rescue the other day? I heard they had to take him to the eye doctor. Yeah, apparently, he kept seeing spots!

Why can't you play cards in the African Savannah? Because there are too many cheetahs!

What did the marksman get when he hit the bullseye?
A very angry bull!

Did you hear about the buffalo that took his boy to school? You know what he said when he dropped him off?
BI-SON!

Why won't leopards ever play hide-n-seek with the other animals?
They're always spotted!

My kitten Meow Meow decided to take a run on the treadmill.

It was a cat-astrophe!

I seeing the poor little guy fly across the room made my wife furry-ous!

I told her the manufacture should have put a warning label on it that it might become a cat-apult!

This joke works best when your delivery is purr-fect!

FAMILY FUN

Lauren, Meow Meow, Aiden & Daddy Duck from the
Towers of Light Series

I told my wife that I always wanted to take her on a date to the moon, but do you know what she said when I told her that?
She said she didn't think it would have any atmosphere.

My family hates it when I sing in the shower. Every now and then I get a little soap in my mouth and all of a sudden, it becomes a soap opera!

My son asked me the other day... "When does a joke become a Dad Joke?" And I said, "When it becomes a-parent!"

So, I asked my wife where she wanted to go on date night. She said, "Anywhere that has seafood." I said, "That sounds kind of shell-fish to me!"

The other day my son asked, "Hey Dad, do you think there's intelligent life on Mars?" And I said, "If there is life on Mars, it's gotta be intelligent because they're not spending billions of dollars to come here."

THE DADA BASE+

My wife sent me out to HomeGoods to buy a new colander. There were so many choices, it just strained my brain!

So, last week I did a talk at a conference trying to help dads out. You know sometimes dads get really busy- Sometimes, we run out of words. I was talking about strategies that dads can use to still connect with their kids and one of them was talking about jokes and the power of dad jokes. Well, I finally got the surveys back. Apparently, my talk was PUN-ishing!

THE DADA BASE+

When I was a kid, my mom used to sprinkle sugar on my pillow before naptime. Yeah, she wanted me to have sweet dreams!

So, it's gotten really snowy here and my wife is tired of it. She wants to see some hummingbirds and some monarchs. So, I threw a stick of margarine out the window. I thought she'd like to see a butter-fly!

We finally got the wedding pictures back from my daughter's wedding. They were just so moving!
The cake was in tiers!

You know, a few minutes before my brother gives me a phone call, I can always sense it.
I have tele-kin-esis!

I've got a buddy whose sister lives in Alaska and is about to give birth to a little girl. My buddy called her up and said, "Hey, you ought to call that little girl brr-niece!"

LAUNDRY

Just had one of my followers ask if I had any laundry jokes. I hate to admit it, but I have loads of them!

So, my wife and I got into an argument over who was going to do the laundry and it just kept piling up and piling up. Finally, I threw in the towel.

This just in from the CDC: Leading cause of dry skin...towels!

You know...if you don't like all these laundry jokes I've been telling. I think you need a dryer sense of humor!

PATRIOTIC

Did you know that the American Flag is the most highly rated flag in the world? Yeah...it's got 50 stars!

Why did Paul Revere ride his horse between Boston and Lexington? Because the horse was too heavy to carry!

Do you know which colonist told the best jokes about King George during the Revolutionary War? The Pun-sylvanians!

You know who got voted to be the funniest person in George Washington's army?
Laf-ayette!

Hey, do you know what's red, white, blue, and green? Uncle Sam after he's been eating that potato salad that's been sitting out all day at the 4th of July party.

Did you hear that they're making the Statue of Liberty a new interactive display?   When you leave, she says, "Stay in torch!"

Did you hear that when the Patriots had the Boston Tea Party they had merch?

Yeah, they were all wearing tea-shirts!

SPORTS & HOBBIES

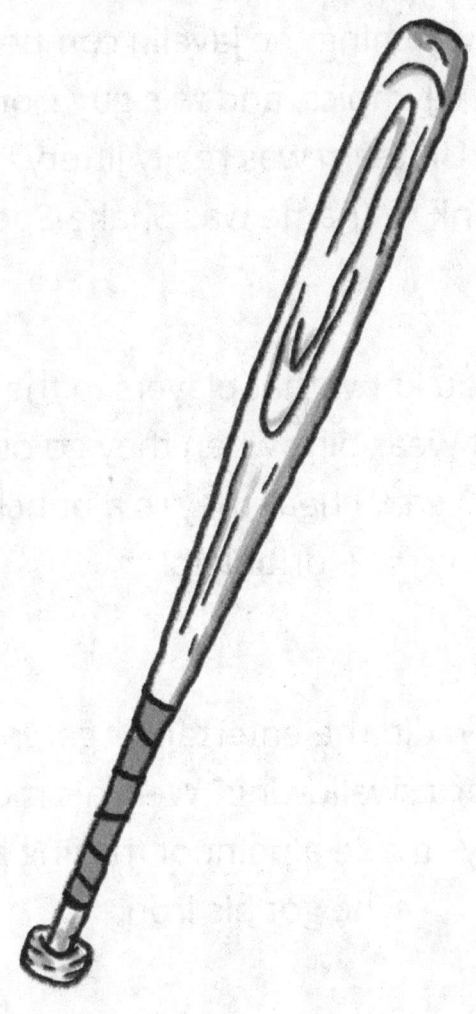

I was watching the javelin competition at the Olympics, and this guy from the UK team was really jittery.
I think his name was Shake-Spear!

Did you know that players in the NBA must wear bibs when they go out to eat? Yeah, I hear they're a bunch of dribblers!

How did the entertainer get into sword swallowing? Well, his mom always made a point of making sure he got his iron.

BIBLE

Quick Bible trivia: What did Samson
from the Bible die from?
Fallen arches!

What do you call a Bible character that
just pulled into the church?
A parking Lot.

If you ever need to build a giant ship
out of gopher wood,
I Noah Guy!

IN THE NEWS

So, I heard they slashed NASA's budget. Now, the sky's the limit!

I hear they've labeled King Tut's tomb as a cybersecurity threat. Apparently, it's un-encrypted.

Did you hear about the girl that got her hair caught in the printing press? It was all over the papers!

Did you know that there is a National Carbonated Beverage with Caffeine Day? You know, as a name for a holiday, I'm not sure it really POPS!

THE DADA BASE+

STAR WARS

You know what the saddest part of
Darth Maul showing up in Solo, A Star
Wars Story, was?
He was just half the man
he used to be.

Did you hear that Chewbacca got
kicked out of Major League Spaceball
for ripping a guy's arms off?
It was a Wookie mistake.

Did you know that the emperor in Star
Wars actually had another apprentice
before Anakin Skywalker? Yeah, he
was a crooked accountant.
Do you know what his name
was? Tax. E. Vader!

Do you know why Darth Vadar's
lightsaber is one yard long?
Because Sith use Imperial units.

Did you know that in the original Star
Wars, there was a scene with Luke and
Aunt Beru where she was
making pickles?
When they finally took it to editing,
they decided they had to cut it out
because it was too
cucumbersome!

Did you see the Easter Egg in the Obi-Wan Kenobi show? Yeah, there was a poster of Obi-Wan Kenobi that said Wanted, Dead or Alive for Grievous bodily harm.

There's been a lot of talk about the IRS doing tax audits lately, so I'm thinking about becoming a Tuskan Raider. They always single-file to hide their numbers.

Do you know what a Stormtrooper's favorite store is?
The one next to Target!

I just heard there's now a support
group for the moms of Stormtroopers.
Apparently, it takes a pretty big toll on
you when your kid always,
misses your birthday.

So, I heard they had to take the Darth
Vader action figure off the market.
Apparently, it was a choking hazard!

Have you ever noticed in Star Wars,
nobody has a pet dog?
I guess people just don't wanna
spacewalk twice a day.

My friend's son Han really appreciates that his parents named him after a Star Wars character. On the other hand, their daughter Chewbacca isn't too happy about it!

Disney is getting really creative with the Star Wars universe. Sounds like they're coming up with all kinds of things. There's this new weapon. It's this energy sword that when you hit somebody with it, it freezes them in carbonite.
I hear they're gonna call it the light sa-brrrrr!

Apparently, my dentist found my TikTok. The last time I was in there when I was getting ready to leave, he said, "May the floss be with you."

Did you know Darth Vadar's bath tub doesn't use water? To protect all of his electrical equipment it's actually crushed up space rocks, it just shoots it out in a fine mist.
Yeah, it's a meteor shower.

Jedi Fun Fact: Did you know that Master Yoda started out on a two-wheeled bike?
He used the do-cycle, cause there is no tri.

My wife and son were headed out to the department of motor vehicles the other day to take him on his driver's test. I handed him a Stormtrooper helmet.

He asked me what it was for.

I said, "So you don't hit anything!"

AUTHOR JOKES

I'm working on a new book
about anti-gravity.
It's going to be a light read!

When my editor read it, she said
it was very uplifting!

My other friend said he

couldn't put it down!

My writing critique group said it was
going to be out of this world!

So, a friend of mine asked me, "Hey, you put out a dad joke every day. Isn't that a lot of hard work?" And I said, "No, not really. I'm just doing it for the pun of it."

What did the sketchbook say to the novel?   I'm drawing a blank!

I had some plans to write a book
about the cause of sinkholes.
But they fell through!

Why can't you go to the world's
biggest library?
It's always overbooked!

Plus it's just exhausting to try to
navigate through it's got
thousands of stories!

A FEW MORE, JUST FOR FUN

So, the kids in my neighborhood have
gotten pretty creative with their
snowmen. We had one out there that
looked kind of like Arnold
Schwarzenegger from the 80s. It had
six-pack abs and everything. I said,
"Hey, what do you call that snowman?"
The kid said, "Abdominal Snowman!"

So, the past, the present, and the
future walked into a bar.
It was tense!

I found this random box of Legos just
sitting at the bottom of my
steps this morning.
I don't know what to make of it!

I talked to the guy who invented the abacus. He said, "It's likely someday that millions of people will have used this device. But, of course, you can never count on these things."

So, you know those lifesaver rings that you see on big ships, ferries, and stuff like that? Apparently, you're not supposed to put them over your head. I guess it kind of makes sense. Who wants "ring around the collar?"

My high school calculus teacher is retiring after fifty years. I wonder how she's doing with the aftermath.

I went out to get the mail today and the snowman across the street asked me for a potato peeler. And I was like, "What? Why?" He said, "Yeah!" He told me he wanted to get a nose job for the ladies!

You can never trust an oak tree...
they are way too shady!

When I tell this joke a lot of people
want to make like a tree and leaf!

I think that's because they must
believe I'm some kind of nut!

Either that or they just don't like a
good pun so
I'm barking up the wrong tree!

TELLING JOKES AND PUNS FOR KIDS

Take the class online for free with code

dadabase

https://www.towersoflight.net/jokeclass

PLAY ON WORDS

Using a common word in a different place than you would expect it to be to provide a clever meaning.

Examples

Why did the tomato turn red?
Because it saw the salad dressing.

How do programmers arrange their crayons?
They use color coding!

What do you call a flower that runs on electricity?
A power plant!

THE DADA BASE+

Match the punchline!

Draw a line to match the opening line on the left to a punchline on the right that would be a good way to play on the opener with the underlined common words.

Opener		Punchline
1. I ate too many gummies the other day.		A. They're going to give him a tough <u>sentence</u>!
2. How much does a rainbow weigh?		B. Apparently, they were having a <u>jam session</u>
3. The world tongue twister champion was recently arrested.		C. <u>On-line</u>
4. Where did the mermaid meet the fisherman?		D. My stomachache was <u>unbearable.</u>
5. I have two printers at home and they were making a ton of noise last night		E. Not much at all, it's <u>pretty light</u>

THE DADA BASE+

Write the opener.

Using the following words with multiple meanings try to think up a joke that uses the expectations of one meaning to make up a joke with the other as a punchline.

___

Bat: A flying mammal or a piece of sports equipment

___

___

Duck: A type of bird or to avoid something

___

___

Fan: A device for moving air or an enthusiastic supporter

___

___

TWIST OF A PHRASE

Using a common phrase in a different place than you would expect it to be to provide a clever twist on that phrase.

Examples

I'm reading a book on anti-gravity.
It's impossible to put down.

Why don't scientists trust atoms?
Because they make up everything.

Why did the scarecrow win an award?
Because it was outstanding in its field.

THE DADA BASE+

Match the punchline!

Draw a line to match the opening line on the left to a punchline on the right that would be a good twist on the opening line

Opener		Punchline
1. Why did the circus lion eat the tightrope walker		A. Because he was an undercover cop!
2. Why was the policeman always taking naps?		B. Because he doesn't like <u>being followed</u>!
3. Why doesn't Pac-Man use Twitter?		C. But now it's a <u>hand's on</u> activity
4. I'm trying to organize a hide and seek tournament		D. He wanted a <u>well-balanced meal</u>!
5. I used to play piano by ear.		E. But it's really <u>hard to find</u> good players

Write the opener.

Using the following punchline think up different openers that would work with the underlined common phrase.

You wouldn't get it.

They stormed out.

Because it's always so overbooked.

FUN WITH HOMOPHONES

A homophone is a word that sounds like another word. Using these words interchangeably can create some really clever punchlines.

Examples:

Why do skunks always celebrate Valentine's Day?
Because they are scent-imental!

Where do waffles go on vacation?
Sandy-Eggo!

Why are asteroids so smart?
They have comet sense!

THE DADA BASE+

Match the punchline!

Draw a line to match the opening line on the left to a punchline on the right that would be a good use of homophones.

Opener		Punchline
1. The baker couldn't stop working overtime		A. They are always pre-paired!
2. I'm on a seafood diet		B. Because they are shellfish!
3. How are socks like scouts?		C. I <u>see food</u> and I eat it
4. Why didn't the cheddar cheese want to get sliced?		D. Because he <u>kneaded dough</u>
5. Why don't clams ever donate to charity?		E. It had grater plans!

Write the dad joke.

Using the following homophones think up a joke where you are using one word instead of another.

_____

Flour / Flower

_____

_____

Right / Write

_____

_____

Pun – have fun with this sound

_____

_____

COMMON THINGS THAT MAKE A JOKE FUNNY

Biological References: Also known as potty jokes, these jokes make light of biological processes that aren't appropriate for polite company.

Superiority: references that help the audience feel like they are more important or better than the focus of the joke.

Incongruity: The punch line seems completely unrelated to the audience's expectations.

Surprise: Catching the audience off guard with a sudden, unexpected event.

Relief: Setting the audience up with something repetitive or boring such that when they get the punchline, they appreciate the joke being over.

ELEMENTS OF A JOKE

The Setup provides the location, people involved, and general premise of the joke, setting expectations for the audience.

The Punchline leverages the everyday things that make a joke funny to delight the audience.

Timing describes the pace at which the joke is told, which allows for anticipation and creates tension, adding power to the punch line.

Delivery refers to your tone of voice, facial expressions, and body language. Varying these while telling the joke helps engage the audience.

THINGS TO AVOID

Homework: Don't make the audience think too hard or try to find meaning in something they are unfamiliar with. That could include jargon, an unfamiliar setting, or a cultural reference they might not know.

Being Offensive: Don't use terminology, phases, or concepts that your audience will find inappropriate. This could be related to a sensitive current event.

Laughing at your own joke: If you laugh at your joke before you get the audience's feedback that it's funny, you hurt your timing and delivery.

PRACTICE FOR A REAL JOKE

The Setup

Who	Mr. Brokken and the Construction Foreman
What	Road construction
Where	In my neighborhood
When	Summer time
Why	Because the construction had been going on forever
How	Tell on Tiktok

Example Intro

So, there was this construction crew that had been in my neighborhood for weeks tearing up the streets. It was super annoying driving around all the little work areas. Finally, they started completely blocking off the street with giant barrels that looked like peanut butter jars.

Put punch in your punchline

When writing out a punchline try putting in notes where you are going to [pause] or use [facial or hand expressions] in the delivery.

Example Punchline

So I asked the construction foreman [pause]

[Put arms out wide] "So what's all the peanut butter for?" [Raise eyebrow and pause]

[Smile big] "I kid you not, he said," [pause]

"In case we have a" [pause] "traffic jam"

THE DADA BASE+

Practice Setup

Who	
What	
Where	
When	
Why	
How	

Intro

_____

Punchline

_____

_____

_____

_____

Homework Check

Will your audience know about the things in your setup?

Does it need everyone to understand jargon or slang to make sense?

Are you using something from popular culture that only a few people know about?

THE DADA BASE+

Practice Setup

Who	
What	
Where	
When	
Why	
How	

Intro

_____

Punchline

_____

_____

_____

_____

Homework Check

Will your audience know about the things in your setup?

Does it need everyone to understand jargon or slang to make sense?

Are you using something from popular culture that only a few people know about?

THE DADA BASE+

Match the punchline!

Opener		Punchline
1. I ate too many gummies the other day.		D. My stomachache was <u>unbearable.</u>
2. How much does a rainbow weigh?		E. Not much at all, it's <u>pretty light</u>
3. The world tongue twister champion was recently arrested.		A. They gave him a really tough <u>sentence</u>
4. Where did the mermaid meet the fisherman?		C. <u>On-line</u>
5. I have two printers at home and they were making a ton of noise last night		B. Apparently, they were having a <u>jam session</u>

THE DADA BASE+

Write the opener.

Using the following words with multiple meanings try to think up a joke that uses the expectations of one meaning to make up a joke with the other as a punchline.

Bat: A flying mammal or a piece of sports equipment

Did you hear about the flying rodent that played for the New York Yankees?

- That Bat could really knock it out of the park.

Duck: A type of bird or to avoid something

Did you hear about the Goose that kept hitting it's head?

- It started to wish it was a duck.

Fan: A device for moving air or an enthusiastic supporter

I barely avoided running into my #1 fan the other day

- The ceiling in my bedroom is really low!

THE DADA BASE+

Twist of a Phrase

Match the punchline!

Opener		Punchline
1. Why did the circus lion eat the tightrope walker		C. He wanted a <u>well-balanced meal</u>!
2. Why was the policeman always taking naps?		A. Because he was an undercover cop!
3. Why doesn't Pac-Man use Twitter?		B. Because he doesn't like <u>being followed</u>!
4. I'm trying to organize a hide and seek tournament		E. But it's really <u>hard to find</u> good players
5. I used to play piano by ear.		D. But now it's a <u>hand's on</u> activity

Write the opener.

Using the following punchline think up different openers that would work with the underlined common phrase.

You wouldn't get it.

Did you hear the one about the un-stamped letter? You wouldn't get it.

They stormed out.

What happened when the weatherman got in a fight with the sportscaster? He stormed out.

Because it's always so overbooked.

Why is it so hard to visit the world's largest library. Because it's so overbooked.

THE DADA BASE+

Fun with Homophones

Match the punchline

Opener		Punchline
1. The baker couldn't stop working overtime		A. They are always pre-paired!
2. I'm on a seafood diet		B. Because they are shellfish!
3. How are socks like scouts?		C. I see food and I eat it
4. Why didn't the cheddar cheese want to get sliced?		D. Because he kneaded dough
5. Why don't clams ever donate to charity?		E. It had grater plans!

THE DADA BASE+

Write the Dad Joke

Using the following homophones think up a joke where you are using one word instead of another.

Flour / Flower

Did you hear about the rose that grew without water?
It must have been a self-raising flower.

Right / Write

Why did the pencil need to go to the ER?
Because the lead broke and it couldn't write itself.

---

pun – have fun with this sound

Did you hear about the superhero whose power is telling Dad Jokes?
Yah, he's the Pun-isher!

For more fun be sure to subscribe at
https://www.towersoflight.net/subscribe

ABOUT THE AUTHOR

Allen Brokken is a teacher at heart, a husband, and a father most of all. He's a joyful writer by the abundant grace of God. He began writing the Towers of Light series for his own children to help him illustrate the deep truths of the Bible in an engaging and age-appropriate way, and has dedicated 15 years of his life to volunteer roles in children's ministry and youth development.

Now that his own children are grown up, he's sharing his life experiences on social media, at home school conferences, and through his blog, occasional cool dad projects, and the Silly Celebrations newsletter at https://towersoflight.net/subscribe

You can get regular sneak peeks of the ongoing adventures of Lauren, Aiden, and Ethan (plus their pets!) and the #dadjokeoftheday on all the major social media platforms. @allenbrokkenauthor

ALLEN BROKKEN'S BOOKS

The Towers of Light series insightfully examines Christian values from the perspective of three small children facing insurmountable problems and succeeding by faith and grace alone.

Book 1: _Light of Mine_- Discernment
The Darkness has taken their parents. Can Lauren, Aiden, and Ethan determine who to trust before it takes them, too?

Book 2: _Still Small Voice_ – Conscience
Lauren, Aiden, and Ethan want to follow their conscience to save their parents, but their uncle has other plans. Will he see the light before it's too late?

Book 3: _Fear No Evil_ - Courage
Lost and alone in a valley of Darkness, will Lauren, Aiden, and Ethan experience God's courage to find redemption–and each other?

Book 4: _Armor of God_ – Faith
Lauren, Aiden, and Ethan race across the Heathlands on a quest to arm themselves with the Armor of God. Will their faith give them the power to save their father?

Book 5: _Wellspring of Life_ – Redemption
Lauren, Aiden, and Ethan must find the legendary wellspring of life. Will they be able to share its living waters before it's too late?

Book 6: _Demolishing the Stronghold_ – Victory
Lauren, Aiden, and Ethan reach Blooming Glen only to find the city defended by the Dark One's Forces. Will they have the faith to overcome the enemy and light the Tower?

**Logan vs. the Hateful Strawberries** Logan finds a secret patch of **strawberries with strange powers**! It makes Logan wonder if these are the fruit of self-control the pastor was always preaching about. Join Logan and his new raccoon friend, Rascal on an adventure to solve the mystery **before Pa gets a chance to turn Rascal into a hat**!

Meow Meow Milks the Cow:
A Towers of Light Read to Me

In God's Creation big help often comes in small packages.